The Man They Killed on Christmas Day

By Catalin Gruia

2013

37-Minutes Publishing

Translated by Andreea Geambasu

Cover design by Tudor Smalenic

Proof reading: by Anca Barbulescu

ACKNOLEDGEMENTS

I would like to express my special appreciation to Andreea Campeanu, Cristian Lascu, Roxana Dobri, George Hari Popescu and Justin Kavanagh for contributing to this book with their sidebars. And to Andrei Pandele – for his amazing photos.

And thanks to my friends Andreea Geambasu, Dragos Margoi, Anca Barbulescu and Tudor Smalenic, Ioana Popescu who encouraged me and helped make this project happen.

CONTENTS

FOREWORD

Ne Sutor Ultra Crepidam!

By Cristian Lascu, Editor In Chief of the Romanian edition of National Geographic Magazine.

"Cobbler, stick to thy last!" master Apelles yelled at a shoemaker who, thinking that he was good at everything, criticized the way the former had painted a sandal. When the smoke of the Ceausescus execution cleared, we were frustrated. Somebody had cheated. Instead of an embarassing crime, there should have been a Nürenberg trial of the communist dictatorship. How is it possible not to repeat mistakes if you do not understand their causes and you do not criticize them openly?

This story about Ceausescu, documented and illustrated brilliantly, brings back memories about the hardships, abuses, and peculiarities of daily life during the dictatorship. Time, however, has blurred the details; what happened then seems incomprehensible for young people, and this dry documentary about Ceausescu may seem too late for them.

On the other hand, through a wide angle lens with a focal range of 25 years, author Catalin Gruia atempts to cover a subject that unfolded over a more-than-50 year range. The distorsions thus become inevitable; history has to be looked at through a telescopic lens. Ceausescu's ascent and decline is long and complicated, but its meaning can be succint: a simple but ambitious man succeeded in holding on to the absolute state power for 25 years.

In all his actions, he was a passionate, consistent communist and patriot, therefore, he was to the liking of the poor, of the mob, and of the nationalists, at least for a while. He entered the arena of politics like a soccer player and the crowd everywhere cheered him on, forgetting that it's no use scoring in an away game if you lose at home.

He wanted to accomplish a lot, he had no education, and being suspicious by nature and hating the elites, he did not even want to listen to those who were knowledgeable. Facing death, he yelled: "Long live the free, independent, Socialist Republic of Romania!" By then, his obsessive dream, the Socialist Romania, was almost built. It had been built, however, on sand, by an exceptional but incompetent dictator.

About this Book

I was just trying to convincingly prove a hypothesis: that Ceausescu's life was a road to hell paved with good intentions.

For me, Ceausescu's death put a serious spanner in the works. I had just won a school contest in speed skating. The prize was a place in a children's mountain camp, which got cancelled because of the events in December 1989.

How could the fall of communism compare to the drama of losing that prize, to my nine-year old eyes?

Oh well, forget about that camp – sour, like any grapes you can't reach. A few days later I went to the grandparents' village, for the yearly slaying of the pig. Then, just at the culmination, when the pig was screeching madly under the knife, its nostrils blowing thick jets of steam, pinned down in the snow by a bunch of men wearing heavy sheepskin coats, the adults let go of the animal and rushed into the house, crowding around the TV.

They came back out after long minutes (I refused to go inside) with their faces transformed with stupefaction mixed with joy, heatedly discussiong the big news. I can't remember exactly when we killed the pig that year, so I can't be sure what the news was: The 22nd of December – the Tyrant's flight from the Central Committee building. The 24th – his apprehension. I remember I started to chant out like an idiot the rhyme I heard on everyone's lips: Olé, olé – Ceausescu nu mai e! (Ceausescu is gone !)

I also remember that only my half-illiterate grandmother remained skeptical in the midst of this general effervescence: „It does not bode well for a people to hunt down its leaders like that".

I understood even less of the happiness of the grown-ups the second or third day after, when I happened to be in front of the TV just when they were broadcasting scenes from the execution of the Ceausescus (after which whoever was directing the live revolution put on some Animal Farm cartoons). To my child's mind, the Ceausescus were just two

9

little old people put against the wall of an outhouse and pierced full of bullet holes on Christmas day.

Fifteen years later, I spent almost 11 months studying Ceausescu's life for a National Geographic documentary. I let his ghost follow me through dozens and dozens of books and interviews – I even dreamed of him at night.

As far as I'm concerned, a story is good as long as it obeys the great rule of any journalistic material: convincingly prove a hypothesis. And my hypothesis for the article in National Geographic was that **Ceausescu's life was a road to hell paved with good intentions.**

I set out in my work without resentment; I associated the last decade of Ceausescu's regime with my beautiful childhood, spent mostly in the countryside, not with what it really was – a black stain of deprivation in Romania's history. I think that may be why I've been able to present Ceausescu objectively, without hating or admiring him, the way you would describe a faraway planet that you look upon detachedly, though a telescope.

But I must confess I enjoyed working on the Ceausescu project because it was easy for me to empathize with the character. I ended up recognizing myself in him: a guy from the village who fails to adapt to the city, lacking culture but intelligent enough to push through, with his failed struggle to overcome his inferiority complexes (turned superiority complexes…)

I've ended up seeing him both as a tyrant with narrow vision and as a victim of an obedient, sycophantic people. Ultimately, I've ended up wondering what would happen to me, or to you, if everyone started to flatter and cajole us year after year, telling we are some sort of Gods.

In a few sentences, Ceausescu's life could be summarized as follows: This is the story of a state resident, for whom the world was a great village. His cottage happened to be Romania. For 24 years he led this country like an ambitious peasant, dreaming of turning an impoverished small holding into a rich farm.

He struggled to earn the respect of the people. Tired of depending on and borrowing money from his affluent neighbors, he tried to make it on his own. At first, he thought he would succeed. But he was sloppy and hasty. What others had, he wanted as well, without thinking too much about feasibility or necessity. If any other two world leaders fought, he would jump in to break them up. For a while he treated his people well – giving them many jobs and houses – but when things stopped going his way, he exploited them without mercy.

CHAPTER 1

The Young Underground Hero?

"I had never heard anything about him" - Constantin Pirvulescu, one of the founders of the Romanian Communist Party (PCR).

A short, stuttering kid left home at 11 to make something out of himself in Bucharest. His parents, peasants from Scornicesti, could barely put food on the table for their 10 children. His father, Andruta, had three hectares of land, a few sheep, and would make ends meet by tailoring. "He didn't take care of his kids; he stole, he drank, he was quick to fight, and he swore..." said the old priest from Scornicesti. His mother was a submissive, hard-working woman. The family slept on benches along the walls of a two-room house. Corn mush was their staple food.

Nicolae went to the village school for four years. The teacher taught simultaneous classes for different years in a one-room schoolhouse. The young Ceausescu did not have books and he often went to school barefoot. An outsider from early on, he did not have friends; he was anxious and unpredictable.

In a then cosmopolitan Bucharest – the first city he had seen – Nicolae moved in with his sister, Niculina Rusescu. Soon, he was sent to serve his apprenticeship at the workshop of shoemaker Alexandru Sandulescu, active member of the Romanian Communist Party (PCR), who initiated his apprentice in conspirative missions. Nicolae did not adapt to Bucharest.

The switch from a world in which he couldn't find his place (his own village) to another in which he still couldn't find his place (the intimidating city) marked him. "His initiation into the marginalized movement of the communists was his alternative solution for integrating into social life," says sociologist Pavel Campeanu, author of the book **Ceausescu: The Countdown**.

Historians of the Golden Age never miss an opportunity to hyperbolize Ceausescu, the activist, as a "young hero," arrested for the first time at the age of 15, and who, by the age of 26, had spent 7 years in prison.

The truth is that, in the 1930s, Nicolae was a rash, incompetent kid. "I had never heard anything about him," says Constantin Parvulescu, one of the founders of the Romanian Communist Party (PCR). He would receive minor missions from his communist bosses. For example, in 1934 in Craiova, with three other young people, he caused a stir at the trial of a group of communists led by Gheorghe Gheorghiu Dej, who was at the time the leader of the Romanian Rail System union in Bucharest. Ceausescu and his comrades were arrested and beaten by the police.

According to the testimony of Ion Gheorghe Maurer, who would become president of the Council of Ministers, Nicolae had been paid to distribute manifestos and petitions just as others were paid to sell newspapers.

Until the mid-1930s, Nicolae traveled on "missions" in Bucharest, Craiova, Campulung, or Ramnicu Valcea. He was arrested several times. His record was beginning to convey the image of a "dangerous communist agitator" and "distributor of communist and anti-fascist propaganda."

His first prison sentence: June 6, 1936, the court of Brasov – two years in prison, plus 6 months for defiance of the court, a 2000-lei fine, and a year of home detention in Scornicesti. The largest part of his sentence was served at Doftana. His fellow inmates say that the prisoner Ceausescu was envious, vengeful, and tough. But he knew how to get under people's skin.

When he got out of prison, Ceausescu was no longer quite as anonymous. He became a leading member of the youth organization of the Romanian Workers' Party (PMR). In Romania, there were about 700 free communists (led by Patrascanu, Foris, Pirvulescu) and about 200 more imprisoned (the generation that had taken part in Dej's railway strike); a royal dictatorship has been instated, activist meetings were rare, money was scarce, member IDs and membership dues did not exist.

He was soon arrested again and sent to Jilava for three years for "conspiring against the social order." Ceausescu spent the war years in prisons and work camps: Jilava (1940), Caransebes (1942), Vacaresti (August, 1943), Targu Jiu (September, 1943).

The bars isolated him from what was happening outside: the agreement between Hitler and Stalin; internal conflicts between communists; the loss of Basarabia and North Ardeal territories; the attempted legionary coup d'etat; the abdication of Carol II; the Antonescu dictatorship. Sealed away from the tumultuous history unravelling in his homeland, the prisoner plotted his own vision for Romania's future.

CHAPTER 2

Butter Up, Fit In, Work, Climb the Ladder

An uneducated young man, but with a real instinct for power

August 1944 was a crossroads in his – and Romania's – destiny: Ceausescu was released and began his rise to power. The Romanian communist family – the Moscovite faction, the imprisoned generation of Dej, and the veteran covert activists – reunited that autumn in the mansion at 16, Eliza Filipescu Lane (where the Indian Embassy is housed today). Ceausescu was among them.

Under the protective wing of Dej, whose favorite he had become while in prison, Ceausescu struggled, flattered, adapted, worked, raised himself up, step by step, tenaciously, stubbornly, and with a real instinct for power:

☐ at 27 he was the leader of the Communist Youth Organization (UTC) and, later, of the Central Committee (CC) of the Romanian Workers' Party (PMR);

☐ at 28 – party instructor in Constanta and Oltenia;

☐ at 29 – deputy in the Grand National Assembly (after he had mobilized motorized troops in the electoral precinct to „convince" electors to place ballots in the urns which had already been filled by the communists ahead of time);

☐ at 30 – Sub-Secretary of State in the Ministry of Agriculture (where the forced collectivization began);

☐ at 31 – Co-Minister of Defense, political head of the army, then politruk with a specialization in Moscow;

☐ at 36 – secretary of the Central Committee (a key position in the Communist Party, dealing with the organization of the Party);

☐ at 37, during the second Romanian Workers' Party congress, he was accepted as a member of the politburo, where his duty was to supervise the

17

internal affairs of the party within the Ministries of the Interior, Securitate, the Armed Forces, the Magistracy, and Justice (he used this position to create a network of connections, installing his people in the Party's key positions).

CHAPTER 3

The Rookie in the Political Office

The honeymoon of the first steps of the youngest ever political leader in Europe

November 5, 1957. An IL-14 airplane carrying a delegation of 14 Romanian Workers' Party members, on its way to Moscow for the October anniversary of the Great Socialist Revolution crashed upon landing at the Vnukovo airport, at 17:48, due to a piloting error. The Foreign Minister, Grigore Preoteasa, and three members of his delegation died. The other passengers suffered serious injuries.

Nicolae Ceausescu, the secretary of the Central Committee of the Romanian Workers' Party, was luckier. The medical record released in Moscow states: „Trauma to the outer right hemithorax and to the left calf. Scratch wounds on the face, hands, and feet. Temperature: 37.5 degrees, general state: satisfactory." But fate had still been close to playing the most cruel joke on this ambitious young man, when he was just steps away from grasping power.

A few years later, on March 19, 1965, 17:45, when Gheorghiu Dej died surrounded by the leading team of the Romanian Workers' Party, Nicolae Ceausescu was the first to bend over and kiss him.

The three veteran members of the politburo, friends of Dej who were qualified to replace him, were not well suited for the job because of their "unhealthy origins": Ion Gheorghe Maurer was German, Emil Botnaras – Ukrainian, Dumitru Coliu – Bulgarian. (According to Paul Niculescu-Mizil, former member of the Central Committee, the three prerequisites for the future leader were: 1. to be Romanian, 2. to be an activist, 3. to be part of the working class).

The desire of this triumvirate of the old guard to promote a docile young man to the head of a collective leadership converted Ceausescu's defects into strengths. They pulled the strings for the junior member of the Politburo whom they considered the easiest to manipulate.

At the congress of July 19 – 24 meant to validate the Politburo elections, the 1357 delegates voted Ceausescu not as Prime Secretary, but as Secretary General, a title not used in the

Eastern Bloc since the death of Stalin. Ceausescu, 47 years old, Europe's youngest political leader to date, launched his mandate at full strength: the PMR returned to its old name, the Romanian Communist Party. After only one month, the name of the country changed too: Romania went from being a Popular Republic to being a Socialist Republic. The honeymoon of the first steps in this seemingly modest and tolerant young dynamo's governing career did not in any way foreshadow the bitter years of its end.

In the beginning, Ceausescu successfully focused on 4 goals:

☐　the liberalization of internal politics;

☐　the wellbeing of Romanians;

☐　more power for himself (under the pretext of rehabilitation for the victims of the Dej period, he pulled the strings to replace the team that had promoted him and with whom he was supposed to share power, with the younger members from his entourage);

☐　an offensive strategy of seduction of the West, playing the rebel son of the Warsaw

Pact family, while careful not to upset the USSR too much.

Romanians lived better and they were proud of their President. Frustrated by history, they saw in Ceausescu one of their own, who was on equal standing with the world's bigger players. When he condemned the military intervention in Czechoslovakia (on the night of August 20-21, 1968), Romanian enthusiasm was spontaneous. This act of defiance against Moscow brought him the respect of the entire world.

But August 1968 was just the tip of the iceberg: Ceausescu consistently cultivated his aura of atypical communist leader:

☐ he was the first to stabilize diplomatic relations with the Federal Republic of Germany (1967),

☐ the only one who did not break off relations with Israel after the Six-Day War (June 1967),

☐ the only head of state who allowed Jewish citizens in his country to leave for Israel (it cost $2,000 - $5,000 per person, as the Securitate general Mihai Pacepa would reveal);

☐　the first Romanian President to visit the United States at a time when relations between the USSR and the US were extremely tense (1970);

☐　the first to refuse to align himself with the oil cartel founded by the General Plan of Comecon (1971),

☐　the leader of the only socialist country that was a member of the World Bank and the IMF (1972), etc.

On March 25, 1974, Ceausescu was elected as the President of the Socialist Republic of Romania, a position especially created for him. The Eastern Block had not seen a communist president before.
Archive photo from Mrs Ioana Popescu personal collection

CHAPTER 4

The Easterns Bloc's Trojan Horse

"In his foreign policy, Ceausescu had a spark of genius" -
Silviu Brucan, former editor-in-chief of Scanteia

I n less than a decade, following the withdrawal of Soviet troops in 1956, the Romania of Gheorghiu Dej went from servility towards Moscow to a more autonomous foreign policy. Dej and his successor, Ceausescu, were both Stalinist wolves who, out of necessity, wore the pro-Western sheepskin of a national-liberal kind of communism, reacting to Khrushchev's attempt to reform the Eastern Bloc.

It was a defensive move that made them as popular at home as they were abroad. The West thought they had found in Ceausescu the Trojan horse of the Eastern Bloc, and they issued him a carte blanche for almost two decades. Some

Western observers exalted him, comparing him to Kennedy or predicting that Romania would become a kind of Switzerland.

His fame as a stubborn, strong-headed nationalist with a special role in the Warsaw Pact opened almost every door for him. And Ceausescu proved to be a born mediator, extremely tolerant in his foreign policy (the polar opposite of the fanaticism that he exemplified in his internal affairs) – he was capable of making a pact with the devil himself.

"Ceausescu was a tyrant when it came to politics, an economic disaster, but in his foreign policy he had a spark of genius," said Silviu Brucan, former editor-in-chief of Scanteia, and later one of the main actors of the events in 1989. "Although uneducated, he was smart, a wily, peasant sort of smart."

Soon, political tourism in Romania was in style. Richard Nixon, the future president of the US, was the one who opened the season in 1967. That year, Corneliu Manescu, the Romanian Foreign Affairs Minister, became the president of the UN General Assembly.

Ceausescu returned the visits. 1973 was the apogee of his trips abroad: Iran, Pakistan, the Netherlands, Italy, the Federal Republic of Germany, Yugoslavia, the US, the Vatican, the USSR, Morocco, and several countries in South America.

Pope Paul VI told him in the Vatican (May 26, 1973): "Excellency, we ask Heaven to bless your activity, which we follow with great interest, and we ask you to consider us humble supporters of your policies of independence and sovereignty, which you are executing with such consistency."

Ceausescu collected a considerable number of friends, medals, orders, and academic titles, a list of which would fill up 30 pages of this book. They vary from the French Legion of Honor to Luxembourg's Order of the Gold Lion of the House of Nassau, from the Order of the White Rose of Finland to the National Order of the Leopard of Zaire, from the British Order of the Bath to a handful of Orders of Lenin, of Karl Marx, and of the Red Banner from communist countries.

He was the contemporary of six American presidents; he got along with all of them, and was friends with Nixon (they visited each other in Washington and Bucharest twice).

Most of the time, he cultivated his good relations with the United States, which were tested in 1970 when Romania suffered floods (38 out of 39 provinces were affected, 600,000 people were evacuated) and America sent more than $11.6 million in aid, and culminated on July 25, 1975 when Romania obtained Most Favored Nation status (renewed annually until 1988).

Moscow had gotten used to the grandeur of Ceausescu's foreign policy: they probably considered him an original, yet harmless, clown. He, however, took himself seriously: in July 1973, at a meeting of the Eastern European Communist Party leaders, the Romanian spoke heresy: he asked for collaboration with the Social Democrats (considered traitors of communism), called for the abolition of the two military blocs – NATO and Warsaw –, defended China in the quarrel with the USSR, and criticized Brezhnev for not doing more to avoid a nuclear war.

International tensions cooled down for a few years, and his double play was no longer necessary: the West discarded Ceausescu. Between 1974 and 1976, Ceausescu only traveled to the West twice. The number of Western visits to Romania decreased as well. In 1974 no one came. Feeling betrayed by the West, Ceausescu turned to the Russians, whom he needed to help turn Romania into a modern, industrialized state.

In a private conversation in August 1976, Erich Honecker, leader of the German Democratic Republic, then on vacation in Crimea, told Leonid Brezhnev, the head of the USSR: "Ceausescu keeps nagging me to go visit Romania. In general he's been acting better than usual. This is good. We'll catch him again in the Warsaw Pact."

During the same period, Ceausescu oriented himself towards the Third World (Africa, South America, the Arab states). He posed – proving his political instinct – as the European promoter of national independence. He approved million dollar credits, considered investments for the future, cooperated in the exploitation of underground riches and the exportation of industrial products and weapons.

CHAPTER 5

Private Life Details

Ceausescu loved playing chess, pool, volleyball, and traveling abroad. He discovered movies when he was in his mid-thirties. He was a huge Kojak fan, and enjoyed watching American detective movies. All his residences had a special projection room. After 1955, he took to hunting.

Nicolae Ceausescu met Lenuta Petrescu in 1939 at a protest at the Workers' Cultural Center. It was love at first sight; Lenuta was young, beautiful, two years older than him, and a member of the Communist youth organization – she was responsible for Sector 2 of Bucharest under her alias, Florica. Seven years later they were married; they would have three children (Valentin, Zoe, and Nicu) and stay together for 50 years.

"They were very close, they held hands. Ceausescu would not disobey her, and she would take great care of him, making sure he ate, had everything he needed and was satisfied. They would eat in the garden and they would have a good time together.

He liked the music of Ioana Radu and Mia Braia and, after they ate, he would sing, they would play backgammon, and she would cheat. He would say: you cheated again, I'm not playing anymore. She would say: come on, Nicu, I won't cheat anymore... And that's how they had their family fun," says Suzana Andreias, head of personnel at the Ceausescu family residence in Snagov for almost three decades.

Ceausescu liked chess, pool, and volleyball. Based on the verse he would read at party Conventions, it seems he read Romanian literature, primarily the poetry of Eminescu.

He was not a picky eater and had rustic tastes. He discovered movies when he was 35 years old. After 1955, he took up hunting, first invited by local party leaders whom he controlled at the time as member of the Central Committee politburo. Since 1965, it became a rule: he would go no Sunday of the season without hunting. In 25 years, he killed over 7,000 animals.

In 1966, after finishing the Academy of Economic Sciences (ASE) in the evening class section, he presented his thesis: "Selected Problems of Romania's Development in the 19th Century." The real author is unknown. Starting in 1968, his speeches were typed; they make up 33 volumes.

In the last 10 years of his life, he suffered from diabetes. As he grew older, he became more and more fearful. From 1972 on, he did not wear any article of clothing for longer than one day. The Fifth Directorate of the Securitate founded a tailor's workshop just for him: it produced office wear, Lenin caps, Mao jackets, English tweed pants, Soviet style heavy padded coats and German style hunting suits.

He was pedantic and obsessed with punctuality. Every morning, at 8.00 sharp, a line of cars escorted him to the office. He ate lunch at 13:00 sharp. He used Badedas shower gel and shaved with Gillette. He liked Odobesti white wine and red sparkling wine.

CHAPTER 6

Romania's Forced Industrialization

Between 1971 and 1975, Romania's GDP registered an annual growth rate of 11.3% that would never be reached again.

B etween 1950 and 1989, and especially after 1965, industrial production in Romania increased by a factor of 44. Ironically, the driving force behind this Stalinist industrialization was a fear of Moscow. Nikita Khrushchev wanted to transform Comecon into a multinational planning organization. Gheorghiu-Dej refused the role of granary for the Warsaw Pact countries, which would have fallen upon Romania, preferring to turn to the forced industrialization of the country.

Ceausescu stepped on the gas, benefiting from his role as "Trojan horse of the East" and taking advantage of Western financing (especially from the US and the Federal Republic of Germany). His authoritarian style of governing transformed Romania from a mainly agricultural country into one that registered production in almost all industrial branches.

In 1973, he approved the founding of joint ventures with the participation of Western capital. From the first year, there were 20 such enterprises. The volume of commercial exchange with the West almost doubled: from 28% in 1965 to 45% in 1974.

Between 1971 and 1975, Romania registered an 11.3% annual increase in GDP, never again surpassed. Whole towns became construction sites, and the propaganda couldn't keep up with the inauguration of factories and plants that popped up like mushrooms after the rain of Western capital.

It was a hasty process though, usually using outdated technology, without taking into account the effectiveness or the cost of further investments. Ceausescu banked on quantity, not quality. He was obsessed with the country's high investment rate – over one third of the national income – which, for him, was "the only remedy against underdevelopment," while industrialization was "a decisive factor for maintaining national independence and sovereignty."

But the economy was not profitable. The state enterprises, most of which were overstaffed, led to poverty, suffering from the diseases of planned economy in its most acute, Romanian form: disorganization, nepotism, corruption, negligence and theft. The average GDP growth rate in Romania decreased from 11.3% (between 1971 and 1975) to 9.6% (1976-1980), then to 1.8% (1981-1982).

Ceausescu initiated a vast program of building blocks of flats for the peasants who had left their villages and came to work into the cities: between 1981 and 1985 only, more than 750,000 apartments with central heating and hot running water were completed. Dozens of soldiers are running around in March 1989, on one of his Pharaonical construction sites, near Piata Muncii (Labour Square).
Photo by Andrei Pandele.

CHAPTER 7

The Rough Years

The generous policy of the '60s and '70s was replaced by a policy of strict austerity in the '80s. There were ration cards for all the basic food categories. Endless queues. Gas and power failures occurred on a daily basis.

T he galloping industrialization lead to a 10% increase in urban population over a decade: in 1977, almost half of Romania's population of 20 million lived in cities.

Collectivization left the village workforce unemployed, while accelerated industrialization created jobs in the city. The state launched an extensive construction program for peasants who had headed to the city in hopes of gaining a better life. For them, the leap from a small room, with one table and benches on which parents, children, and grandparents slept, to apartments with bedroom, dining room, kitchen and bathroom was real and can be considered one of Ceausescu's accomplishments.

Apartment blocks were built in great numbers: from 1981 to 1985, 750,000 apartments with central heating and hot water opened their doors to their occupants. Between 1965 and 1970, migration from the country to the city as a side effect of industrialization was considered a phenomenon to be desired. In only a few years, because of the imbalance created by this migration, restrictions were put into place for those who wanted to settle in the big cities.

Forced industrialization plunged Romania into debt. Between 1971 and 1982 the foreign debt grew from $1.2 billion dollars to almost $13 billion.

The oil crisis of 1978-1981 was like an earthquake for this economy built on sand. In 1982, Romania's foreign trade income decreased by 17% compared to the previous year. Ceausescu found himself in the situation of not being able to pay back his Western creditors. The country's inability to pay was formally declared. Disgusted by his Western friends, Ceausescu ordered the foreign debt to be paid without taking out new loans. This was another proclamation of national independence, his obsession. Seven years later, Romania was out of debt, paying the price with unprecedented poverty.

In 1984 the Danube – Black Sea canal was inaugurated, after 9 years of construction. The canal, which measures 64 kilometers (40 miles) and shortens the trip to the Black Sea by 400 kilometers (248 miles), had too high taxes to be attractive for navigators ($1 for every ton of cargo) and was yet another act asserting independence from the USSR, with whom Romania shared the Danube Delta.

Construction on the People's House, which was to become the headquarters of the Party and seat of the Government, began in 1985. The head architect, Anca Petrescu, had a team of 400 architects under her direction. Three neighborhoods were leveled – Uranus, Antim, and part of Rahova, along with 17 churches. Every day, over 20,000 builders worked in three shifts. Within five years, the second largest administrative building in the world (second only to the Pentagon outside of Washington, D.C.) rose from the ground with a volume of 2,500,000 cubic meters (88,287,000 cubic feet) and over 7,000 rooms, some of them the size of stadiums. The bill: circa $2 billion.

The grandeur of his economic plans, his obsession with paying off the national debt and his ignoring of the consumer needs of his population all pushed Ceausescu toward a reckoning. Catastrophe was not far off.

The generous politics of the '60s and '70s were replaced by one of strict saving in the '80s. Standing in line to buy food became the public occupation. Buildings had central heating, but it was no longer used; medical assistance was free, but it was lacking medicine and technology, and the doctors took bribes.

The population's energy consumption was reduced by 20% in 1979, 20% in 1982, 50% in 1983, and another 50% in 1985, each measurement based on the already reduced numbers of the previous years.

In 1981, food rationing was reintroduced. There were ration cards for oil, milk, butter, and sugar. The meat on the market was whatever had been rejected for export. Between 1985 and 1988 food exports doubled. To mask the food crisis, Iulian Mincu, Ceausescu's personal doctor, invented a rationed diet plan on the grounds that it was not healthy for an adult to consume more than 3,000 calories per day. In 1983, Ceausescu went even further below his nutritionist's recommendations, fixing per capita rations: 39.12 kg of meat, 73 kg of milk and dairy products, 42.54 kg of potatoes, 66.08 kg of vegetables, 27.49 kg of fruit. Students, teachers and soldiers were forced to participate in agricultural work.

In 1984, the energy crisis started: enterprises were closed due to lack of electricity and raw materials; electricity, gas, streetlights, and heat were cut off daily; gas had become a rarity; on Sundays, driving was limited (one Sunday was only for cars with even-number license plates, the next – only for odd numbers).

In 1985, Mikhail Gorbachev, newly elected Secretary General of the Politburo of the Communist Party of the Soviet Union (CPSU), compared the Romanian economy to an "old horse ridden by a cruel horseman." Romanians were doing badly: only 5% of the population had cars, 19% had TVs, 14.7% had washing machines, and 17.6% had refrigerators. Ceausescu was familiar with the numbers of his weak economy. After 1989, at one of his beachside villas, two versions of documents detailing the last harvests were found, one with the real numbers and the other with the fabricated numbers for propaganda.

According to German-Romanian author Richard Wagner, who left the country in the '80s, "the only people left in his entourage were relatives, lackeys, and criminals ready to do anything. They ran the country like a bunch of demented leaseholders."

CHAPTER 8

The Cult of Personality

"We love him because he has hunger in his heart/For work, so that we may have a better life/All our voivodes hold his arm tightly/And all our forefathers whisper words of wisdom in his ear/He is a man like any other, a man, a man, the man..." from Homage for Ceausescu's 60th birthday, by poet Adrian Paunescu

The cult of personality inflated as reality worsened. In 1980, when the "Year of the Dacians" was celebrated, Ceausescu himself was celebrated as a descendent of Burebista's legacy.

On TV, there were only two hours of broadcast: between 8.00 and 10.00 P.M. Here is a list of programs from January 26, 1987: 8 o'clock – news, 8:20 – "We Praise the Leader of the Country – Poems, an Anthology of Venerations; 8:40 – "A Documentary Devoted to the Theoretical Activity of

Comrade Nicolae Ceausescu," 9 o'clock – "The Veneration of the Supreme Commander," a made-for-TV play accomplished with the help of the artistic assembly of the army; 9:30 – news, end of broadcast.

In November 1984, the penultimate Romanian Communist Party (PCR) Convention was held. Hunger haunted the country, while in the convention room, Nicolae Ceausescu, interrupted by ovations – "Ceausescu – heroism, Romania – communism! Our esteem and our pride, Ceausescu Romania!" – reported on the "strong development of the food industry" to his party members.

This cult of personality started in 1970-1973 with his visit to Asia. Inspired by Mao Zedong in China and Kim Il Sung in North Korea, Ceausescu presented his theses on his own small cultural revolution in July 1971, "with the aim of forming a new kind of man," through which he sought to transform Romania into a Korean-style beehive.

The bees didn't let out the slightest buzz. In 1910, academic Constantin Radulescu Motru wrote: "Romanians have a herd instinct and mimic everything they see around them, like sheep."

On March 25, 1974, Ceausescu was elected President of the Socialist Republic of Romania, a position created especially for him. The Eastern Bloc had never seen a communist

President before. Ceausescu had become an institution: he was the President par excellence - of the State, of the State Council, of the National Defense Council, of the United Socialist Front, of the Supreme Council of Economic and Social Development, of the Permanent Bureau of the Executive Political Committee, of the Ideological Commission of the Romanian Communist Party, and other commissions and committees.

In 1968, when he condemned the invasion of Czechoslovakia, Romanians spontaneously praised him. Immediately, at the 10th Romanian Communist Party convention, his yes-men brought him homage, which he rejected: "We do not need idols or flag wavers. We do not need to make standard bearers out of people. Our idol is Marxism-Leninism and its concepts about the world and the life of the proletariat."

After his visits to China and North Korea, he changed his tune. His election to the position of president meant the beginning of probably the most shameless cult of personality in Europe since Hitler and Mussolini. Ceausescu became an idol in only a few years; he was no longer just the Comrade but titan among titans, the Oak from Scornicesti, strategist of luck, guarantor of Romania's richness, sun, the measure of all things, hawk, the Transfagarasan of our soul, the best worker/soldier/peasant/miner/railway worker /hunter of the country, all-knowing, beloved leader, earthly god, prince charming, the peak that rises above the country, beloved father.

Since 1970, Romanians, predisposed to accepting authoritarian forms of government, participated, at least formally, in the leader's cult. The cult quickly developed its own dynamic, at first a snowball – the nucleus made up of toadies he had resisted several years earlier – that rapidly began rolling, growing with opportunism and the herd mentality, until it finally reached its extreme form in the '80s, becoming a sort of schizophrenia shared by the entire population. His birthday became a national holiday. On each of his birthdays, a new Homage program would come out, heavy with praise and anthems.

"We love him because he has hunger in his heart/For work, so that we may have a better life/All our voivodes hold his arm tightly/And all our forefathers whisper words of wisdoms in his ear/He is a man like any other, a man, a man, the man..." read the Homage for Ceausescu's 60th birthday, by the regime's number one poet, Adrian Paunescu, a Social Democratic Party (PSD) senator in the post-communist regime.

In an interview with his French biographer, Michel-Pierre Hamelet, Ceausescu defined the personality cult organized around him in Romania as „a problem of organization and clear-sightedness."

One last protest: 83 year-old Romanian Communist Party veteran Constantin Parvulescu stood up in the middle of the 7th Romanian Communist Party convention in November 1979 and stated that he did not support Ceausescu, whom he accused of putting his own interest above that of the Party. It was an isolated incident: the leader was reelected and 80,000 Bucharestians gathered for a mega-rally. Students got the day off, and enterprises halted work.

Starting with 1970, Romanians had been - at least on a formal level - involved in Ceausescu's cult. Following his election as a president, the leader's cult - fed by opportunism and herd instinct - quickly developed a dynamics of its own.
Omagial illustration from Mrs Ioana Popescu personal collection.
* I was unable to find the name of the artist who did this collage.

CHAPTER 9

Towards a Potemkin Romania

Surrounded by hypocrites, Ceausescu lost all sense of limitations, and took increasing delight in his role as a feudal despot.

Visits around the country made Ceausescu popular in the first years of his government. Then, local activists started building Potemkin villages for him. Before his arrival, a commando would mask reality: healthy cows popped up in the landscapes, pine trees on the side of the road, apples were tied onto trees with wires, and plastic grapes topped the tables at exhibitions. Everything he said was taken as a valuable order to be executed in full.

For example, in the 80s, when he found out that Westerners were producing huge quantities of corn per hectare

46

(the secret being the production density of 50 – 60,000 plants per hectare), Ceausescu brought the task back to Romania.

One fall, in a county in Transylvania, the comrade visited a representative farm unit. Since they had not been able to achieve the desired density on any field, local specialists stuffed the lot with corn cobs cut from another field.

Excited by the explanations given to him on the side of the field where an exhibition of produce, display boards, and graphics had been strategically placed, Ceausescu walked onto the field, peeled a corn cob, and ended up with one of the cobs that had been put there for show in his hand. He realized it had been a farce, he huffed and puffed, and then he forgot about it.

Surrounded by hypocrites, Ceausescu lost all sense of limitations, and increasingly took delight in his role as a feudal despot.

French president Valéry Giscard d'Estaing, who visited Romania in March 1979, found a Ceausescu who was "arrogant, disagreeable, and surrounded by corrupt idiots." Ceausescu lived his whole life in fear that all those around him could betray him. After Pacepa's flight, his distrust of his close collaborators increased.

He turned to all kinds of solutions: he took the reins of the Party and promoted his relatives to key positions. In time, he dismissed almost all of his intelligent and upright collaborators. The noose of power tightened more and more. His most trusted advisors, who had fought each other to get ahead, competed in shielding him from unpleasant information.

The Second Office, lead by his wife, filtered all information that reached him. Slowly, the court of Bucharest was overrun by an elite of servants who didn't have the courage to tell him the truth, even at the bitter end.

CHAPTER 10

Elena Ceausecu: Romania's Lady MacBeth

Labeled by many as an ill-fated Lady MacBeth figure, Elena Ceausescu became in 1982 the first woman vice president in the history of Romania. Her own personality cult was also initiated on a huge scale.

Elena Ceausescu became number two in the government, the first female vice president in Romania. Born Petrescu on November 17, 1916 in Petresti, Dambovita, daughter of peasants, Elena did not finish fourth grade. She made it to Bucharest where she worked in a textile factory, and met Nicolae in 1939.

Considered by many a fatal Rasputin, Ceausescu's wife collected academic titles and bylines for books written by others. "His biggest mistake was that he listened too much to what mother told him. Even a history written today should point out that mother had an ill-fated influence over him," said the son Nicu Ceausescu in 1991 in Jilava prison, in an interview with writers George Galloway and Bob Wylie.

Elena became interested in politics in 1972. In 1985, her own massive personality cult began.

"In his egomaniacal evolution, Nicolae Ceausescu was, first of all, supported by his wife Elena. She successfully played several roles in his life. On the one hand, she became his surrogate mother taking the place of a real mother who, in the reality of his emotional life, never supported him enough.

Elena succeeded in protecting her husband, accepting him for what he was. But she nurtured a relationship of sick and immature dependency within the couple. She would take care of his health; she would make sure he ate and felt well. She helped him control his stuttering. Throughout these actions, however, she would satisfy her need to control their relationship. She would often manifest this control through the decisions that were made. Nicolae had given her so much power that, towards the end of the Golden Age, she was the one making all the decisions", says psychologist Roxana Dobri.

CHAPTER 11

The Beginning of the End

According to Mikhail Gorbachev, newly elected Secretary General of the Politburo of the Soviet Union's Communist Party (CPSU), in 1985, the Romanian economy was like an "old horse ridden by a cruel horseman".

After the Russian invasion of Afghanistan in 1979, Ceausescu once again got into the good graces of the West. He started getting state visit invitations and he was visited as well. In November 1980, he raised the bar at the CSCE conference in Madrid, presenting his plan for a united Europe, from the Pyrenees to the Carpathians, a common European home without the USSR.

In 1982, Leonid Brezhnev, leader of the USSR, died. For two years he was replaced by Yuri Andropov, who was 68 years old, a former KGB head, lover of reform, and who didn't see Ceausescu with good eyes. Andropov was succeeded by 73 year-old Constantin Chernenko who was insignificant, senile, very much to Ceausescu's taste.

During this period of Moscow's increased weakness, Ceausescu let himself be talked into extending the Warsaw Pact, having claimed that NATO and Warsaw both seemed unnecessary to him. Furthermore, in 1984, Romania was the only country in the Eastern Bloc that participated in the Summer Olympics in Los Angeles.

Unfortunately for Ceausescu, in March 1985, Chernenko was replaced by the dynamic reformer, Mikhail Gorbachev. It was the beginning of the end for Ceausescu and the socialist camp.

In March 1986, Gorbachev presented his perestroika and glasnost theses to the 27th Communist Party of the Soviet Union (PCUS) convention in Moscow. "The actions of the Party's organizations and of the State have fallen behind the times. Indolence, the rigid method of governing, low productivity, a growing bureaucracy, all of these have cost us greatly," he said. He continued, offering up ideas for which Ceausescu had fought all his life: "Each nation should choose its own path and decide the fate of its own territory and resources."

Ceausescu "the dissident" saw his role as Trojan horse usurped. He, who had been the favorite child of the West, found himself falling in their general disfavor. "Betrayed" by the West for the third time, Ceausescu once again turned his back on them, fighting tenaciously against the reforms that threatened his socialist world. But he became more and more isolated. Soon he had only one friend – the other old man of communism, the German Democratic Republic's Erich Honecker. For them, the reforms in Poland and Hungary were a nightmare, and they were the only ones to praise the repression of democratic demonstrations in China in June 1989.

Between the 25th and 27th of May 1987, Mikhail Gorbachev and his wife Raisa came to Romania. A pompous welcome was prepared for them. Hundreds of thousands of people lined up along the side of the road from the airport to the prepared residence. On the last evening, the Ceausescus had dinner with the Gorbachevs in a distinctive atmosphere. The men ended up arguing. Ceausescu told Gorbachev that he would be better off quitting international politics and worrying about the internal problems of the USSR. Gorbachev accused him of keeping his country in a state of fear after having isolated it from the world.

Also in 1987, "Red Horizons," the confessions of one of Ceausescu's lieutenants and the Securitate General, Mihai

Pacepa, was published. Ronald Regan, the President of the United States, called it „my Bible for relations with communist dictators." Radio Free Europe broadcast "Red Horizons," in episodes, bringing the scandals of the Ceausescu household into Romanian homes.

CHAPTER 12

Between Security and Paranoia

According to Securitate general Mihai Pacepa, each officer had to have 50 collaborators (members of the Romanian Communist Party) and 50 informants (outside of the Romanian Communist Party). The result was constant surveillance of the population.

Pacepa's betrayal, in July 28, 1978 caused a stir in the Securitate. Ninety percent of the Romanians who worked abroad were spies. Now, they were in danger. Ceausescu was livid. Pacepa made his secrets public, describing him as "a pygmy in a perpetual state of agitation who would grimace in order to hide his stuttering, spitting on those around him when he spoke. He would only shake his inferiors' hands with three weak fingers, while his eagle eye sized them up." Heads rolled not only in the Securitate (all those who had had connections with Pacepa), but also in related fields. The entire Foreign Intelligence Service was restructured. Pacepa's reasons for deserting remain unclear, but it seems that he had heard that he would be accused of corruption. He fled to the US and the CIA took care of him.

On March 10, 1989, the New York Times published the Letter of the six communists of the old guard: Constantin Parvulescu, Gheorghe Apostol, Corneliu Manescu, Silviu Brucan, Grigore Raceanu, and Alexandru Barladeanu, in which they asked Ceausescu to change his domestic policies. They blamed him for not respecting the Constitution, for his village-urbanization program, for building the People's House, for his repressiveness in domestic policy, and for ruining the national economy. "The conspirators" (whose average age was 80) were placed under house arrest.

On October 25, 1989, Gennadi Gerasimov, spokesman of the Foreign Minister of the USSR, announced a switch in doctrine, from the Brezhnev doctrine to the Sinatra doctrine ("I did it my way"). The events in Eastern Europe quickly came tumbling down: the Berlin wall fell (November 10), Todor Jivkov was dethroned in Bulgaria (November 10), the "citizen's forum" was founded in Czechoslovakia (November 20). In Romania, at the 14th Romanian Communist Party convention (November 22-24), all was well. Ceausescu's five-hour speech was interrupted 55 times by comrades who stood up to applaud him.

On December 4th, Ceausescu left for Moscow in an attempt to save himself. Gorbachev couldn't stand the arrogant Romanian. "His lips were perpetually smirking to show his conversation partner that he could read his thoughts and that he did not value him. This impertinence and his lack of value for others took on a grotesque form over the years. He transferred these traits, maybe without realizing it, from his courtiers to his partners who usually were the same rank as him or higher," wrote Gorbachev in his memoirs.

Old Ceausescu returned home and began preparing to defend his power. His plans for suppressing a coup d'etat, kept in his drawer, were known only by a restricted circle. Work on these plans had begun back in the 70s. Two days after he gave a speech condemning the suppression of the Prague Spring, Ceausescu met with Josip Broz Tito, who told him: "For your own safety, be careful in Romania."

Ceausescu was afraid that the Russians would come after him: he requested safe houses and escape routes, and a radio transmitter to be able to address his people from any location. In 1970, a special unit of the Securitate came up with a secret plan, Rovine IS-70, which involved an escape abroad in case of emergency. At first, the Securitate oversaw the

communist leadership and foreign visitors. Its tentacles
extended throughout the whole country, as Ceausescu grew
older and more paranoid.

In 1965, there was a central phone-tapping center and
11 regional ones. Thirteen years later, there were 248 centers
and 1,000 portable stations. By the 1980s, the Securitate had
become one of the most feared secret police organizations in
the world. In 1989 it had 14,259 employees, of which 8,159
were officers. According to Pacepa, each officer had to have 50
collaborators (members of the Romanian Communist Party)
and 50 informants (outside of the Romanian Communist Party).
The result was the constant surveillance of the population.

In 1971, after a visit to China, Ceausescu called for the
establishment of U.M.0920, a special counter-informative unit,
whose mission was to protect him against a Soviet coup d'etat.
This unit found out about the Dniester operation, initiated in
July 1969, a few days after which, contrary to Moscow's
recommendation, Ceausescu visited Nixon. Brezhnev, irritated
by Ceausescu's nationalism, considered replacing the
Romanian.

By 1978, U.M.0920 had identified nine Army and
Securitate generals whom the Russian First Chief Directorate
(PGU) wanted to use in a coup d'etat against Ceausescu.
According to Pacepa, many agents recruited by Moscow from

the Romanian Communist Party for the Dniester operation were released of their duties, and then repeatedly rotated lest they take political roots or be contacted by Soviet informants.

Also according to Pacepa, the highest ranking victim of U.M.0920 was Ion Ilici Iliescu, one of Ceausescu's favorites. Ruling over the party's vast propaganda machine and national misinformation operations, Iliescu was an intelligent young man who had studied in Moscow, gaining a thorough Marxist education. Ion Iliescu was named Ilici after Vladimir Ilici Lenin, whom his extremist father idolized. Pacepa says Iliescu preferred not to report to his mentor an allusion made by a member of an "ideological" delegation (and recorded on tape), according to which "the Kremlin would be happier with Iliescu as the head of the Romanian Communist Party." In Iliescu's version, Ceausescu would have dismissed him because he had not agreed with his "little cultural revolution."

Other victims of U.M.0920: Valter Roman (father of Petre Roman, the future Prime Minister) and Silviu Brucan.

CHAPTER 13

"Down with Ceausescu!" The Turning Point in Timisoara

On December 17, the Army opened fire on the crowd in Timisoara.

On December 16, 1989, the Timisoara revolt began. 1,000 people gathered in the center of town, shouting "Down with Ceausescu". A state of emergency was declared. In the middle of the crisis, Ceausescu accused Army and Securitate generals: "You should be sent before the execution squad. That's what you deserve, because what you have done means fraternizing with the enemy."

Tired and disappointed, Ceausescu threatened to resign. A wave of cries from the Central Committee members for him to change his mind followed; a few women broke down in tears. In the end, Elena persuaded him.

"OK, shall we try again, comrades?" he asked those around him. Before leaving for Iran, he forbade anyone from entering the country if they were not from North Korea, China, or Cuba, convinced that the coup d'etats that had taken place in the German Democratic Republic, Bulgaria, and Czechoslovakia were due to outside help. On December 17, the platoons fired at random into the crowd. The next day, it was quiet in a city under siege.

CHAPTER 14

The Execution Squad

"When he fell, he cried, 'Long live the free and independent Socialist Republic of Romania!'- Andrei Kemenici, commander of the Targoviste garrison.

On December 20, Ceausescu held a telephone conference with the secretaries of each county: he told them that spies were working in Timisoara, accusing the US and the USSR of having made an agreement regarding Romania. That evening on TV, he told the country about the hooligans in Timisoara.

The next day, he called a meeting in Bucharest where he promised an increase in salaries and rations. He was booed. The people came out to protest in Bucharest, too. Barricades. The army fired. On December 22, 162 people had already died. The day after the failed meeting in Bucharest, the masses gathered once again in front of the Central Committee, where the Ceausescus had remained overnight. In the morning, the Minister of Defense, Vasile Milea, was found dead in his office.

Ceausescu once again appeared on the balcony before the crowds. Booing ensued again. General Stanculescu, newly appointed Minister of Defense, called a helicopter, pleading with his President to leave the Central Committee building.

"I warned my father that this moment would come and that it would happen this way. The night before he was overthrown, I talked to him for approximately 15 minutes. I implored him to make concessions, to welcome a people's delegation. He was listening but not hearing. Mother told me: Don't be a fool. He always listened to Mother too much," said his son, Valentin Ceausescu to writers George Galloway and Bob Wylie.

The Ceausescu regime's movie was reaching a surrealistic end, and the reel was turning faster and faster. The Ceausescus took the elevator up to the roof. The doors were blocked before the last floor. The bodyguards opened them with blows of their weapons. They climbed onto the Central Committee terrace through a window.

They flew to Snagov, where Ceausescu tried to get in touch with the Government, the Army, and the Securitate.

Nobody answered. They continued on in the helicopter. The pilot warned them that they could be shot down. They landed on the road in Titu. They stopped a red Dacia, which took them to the village of Vacaresti. They took another car to Targoviste. They stopped at the Aggregate Works of Special Steel where Ceausescu wanted to talk to the workers. They didn't open the gates for him.

They went on to the Center for the Protection of Plants in Targoviste. A Militia team came and escorted them to the Inspectorate. The building was surrounded by an angry mob. The Militia car was attacked with stones and followed by several other cars. They fled the city with the two militiamen and hid in the forest near Ratoaia, 20 km outside Targoviste. Only at night were they brought into the Militia building.

Some soldiers took them to the barracks in a white Aro car; they were given military clothes and they were locked in a small, unventilated room. Although they still called him "comrade President," "comrade Supreme Commander," his tea was sweetened with sugar even though he was a diabetic. Ceausescu was furious. Elena caressed him like a child. On the first night, they slept in the same bed, embracing, and constantly whispering to each other. In the following days, they were locked in a bulletproof TAB vehicle (for their safety, they were told), where they spent their last night.

The former major lieutenant, Iulian Stoica (today an Army Reserve Major), guardian of the Ceausescus between December 22nd- 25th in the Targoviste garrison, recounts in a TV interview how, on the 24th of December, Ceausescu verbally attacked his wife (they usually got along very well and took care of each other) when he heard the names of the protagonists of the tele-revolution of 1989.

(Stoica had gone out for tea, and he got stuck for 30 minutes in front of the TV that showed incredible things. He told them that he had seen Mircea Dinescu, Sergiu Nicolaescu, Ion Iliescu, etc. in studio 4. Elena, who had the best information cadre, insulted each one of them.) When he heard Ion Iliescu's name, Ceausescu stood up, and started yelling at Elena: "You didn't let me. You didn't let me do what I should have done. You will see, now he will finish us off, that Soviet spy."

"It was the first time the two of them had had a confrontation and a heated discussion," says Stoica. He goes on to say that on the night of December 24th, he thwarted four assassination attempts against the Ceausescus, ordered by colonel Kemenici in hopes of avoiding the embarrassing trial that would follow the next day.

Two days after fleeing from the Central Committee building, several members of the National Salvation Front's inner circle gathered around Ion Iliescu in a bathroom at the Ministry of Defense, turned on the faucets so that no one could hear them, and decided what to do with the Ceausescus.

On December 25th, General Victor Stanculescu, with a suite of military personnel and civilians, landed in Targoviste in a helicopter.

When Ceausescu saw him, he let out a sigh of relief. "Don't worry," he told Elena, "Stanculescu is here!" Little did he know that the man whom he had named Minister of Defense a few days earlier had betrayed him and had come to prepare his death. The Ceausescus' trial was a masquerade in which even the defense attorneys tried to out-accuse the prosecution. The presidential couple was sentenced to death and lined up with their backs against one of the outhouses in the unit.

Andrei Kemenici, commander of the Targoviste garrison, who had been promoted to General in the meantime (all those who had contributed to this trial were to be rewarded by the new regime), declared in an interview 10 years after the trial: "the hardest part was when I saw the paratroopers trying to tie up Nicolae and Elena.

She was begging for mercy and struggling. He didn't struggle. He endured the humiliation. But tears were running down his cheek. He was sobbing. No, he was no longer Ceausescu, he was just a man, and when he was riddled with bullets, I broke down in tears. When he fell, he yelled, 'Long live the free and independent Socialist Republic of Romania!' I don't know if the communist heroes yelled out slogans as they died, as literature would have us think, but Nicolae Ceausescu died exactly like in those books, like in the movies."

TIMELINE

"The Golden Age" Of Nicolae Ceausescu

The rise and fall: 25 years of communist reign

Four major steps in domestic policy:

☐   The Thaw (1965-1969)

☐   Cultural Revolution (1970-1973)

☐   Romanian Neo-Stalinism (1974-1979)

☐   Decade of Crisis (1980-1989)

Four major steps in foreign policy:

☐   Western political tourism in Romania (1965-1974)

☐   Reorientation towards the USSR and Third World countries (1974-1977)

☐   Rapprochement with the West (1978-1984)

☐   Anti-perestroika resistance and total isolation (1985-1989)

Timeline

1965 – Nicolae Ceausescu, Secretary General of the Romanian Communist Party at 47, is Europe's youngest political leader to date.

1966 – A series of laws prohibit abortion and contraceptives; divorce procedures become more difficult.

1967– Corneliu Manescu, Romanian Foreign Minister, becomes president of the UN General Assembly; Richard Nixon becomes the first in a series of Western guests to visit Ceausescu during the Cold War.

1968 – Defying Moscow, Ceausescu condemns the interference of the Warsaw Pact troops in Czechoslovakia. Wave of enthusiasm in Romania. Western interest in "the Trojan horse of the Eastern Bloc"; hypocritical plan of rehabilitation of Dej regime victims, meant to isolate those who propelled him to power.

1970 – Catastrophic floods in Romania, 38 out of 39 counties affected, 600,000 people evacuated.

1971 – Ceausescu visits Mao Zedong in China and Kim Il Sung in North Korea. He begins to model his cult of personality after theirs; road signs bearing Transylvanian town names in Hungarian and German are prohibited.

1971-75 Romania achieves a GDP growth rate of 11.3%, never again surpassed.

1972 – Romania becomes the only socialist country to become a member of the World Bank and the IMF; Ceausescu meets Anwar Sadat, Yasser Arafat, and other members of the Organization for the Liberation of Palestine in Cairo, and begins peace talks concerning war in the Middle East.

1973 – The apogee of foreign visits: Iran, Pakistan, the Netherlands, Italy, the Federal Republic of Germany, Yugoslavia, the USSR, several South American countries, Morocco, the US, the Vatican; Romania allows the founding of joint ventures with the participation of Western capital (51% Romanian capital).

1974 –Ceausescu is elected President of the Socialist Republic of Romania, a position created especially for him; State monopolies seize all rare metals and precious stones.

1974-1976 – The West gives up on Ceausescu, who travels there only twice. He reorients himself towards the USSR and the Third World, where he plays the role of credit-lending European.

1975 – Romania obtains Most Favored Nation status with the US (renewed yearly until 1988)

1976 – The right of settlement in big cities is heavily limited.

1977 – In March, a 7.9 magnitude earthquake: 1,570 dead, 11,300 injured, 35,000 households destroyed; in August, the Jiu Valley miners' strike; in October, the new anthem of the Socialist

Republic of Romania. (based on a text by Ceausescu) and the law that replaced "Mister," "Mrs.," "Sir," and "Ma'am" with "comrade" or "citizen."

1978 – The Ceausescus visit Great Britain (June 13-16); the betrayal of the general of the Securitate, Mihai Pacepa (July 28). Foreign Intelligence Service restructured.

1979 – At the 7th Romanian Communist Party (PCR) Convention in November, Constantin Parvulescu, veteran of PCR, 83 years old, rebukes Ceausescu for placing his personal interest above those of the party; cars can be driven every other Sunday, alternating even and odd license plate numbers; The Russian invasion of Afghanistan; Ceausescu is again esteemed by the West.

1979-1981 – The fall of the Shah of Iran; the oil crisis strikes countries with unstable economies, like Romania.

1980 – CSCE conference in Madrid in November: Ceausescu presents his plan for a united Europe, from the Pyrenees to the Carpathians; a person may not be in possession of more than one house or apartment.

1981– Rationing of staple foods. Drastic measures for energy savings. Gas is scarce; people forced to participate in agricultural work.

1982 – Ceausescu orders the rapid payment of foreign debt (almost $13 billion) without taking out new loans. Romania under austere measures without precedent; emigrants' houses and land taken by the state.

1983 – Possession of photocopiers prohibited.

1984 – The Danube – Black Sea canal is inaugurated, after 9 years of construction; any privately owned typewriter must be registered with the Militia; energy crisis; new legal, fiscal, and medical rules for a more efficient enforcement of anti-abortion laws; Romania is the only Eastern Bloc country to participate in the Summer Olympics in Los Angeles despite the Soviet boycott.

1981-1985 – 750,000 apartments opened for use; the inhabitable surface area per capita is 12 m2.

1985 – Construction begins on the People's House, which was to become the headquarters of the Party and seat of the Government; any conversation between a Romanian and a foreigner must be reported to the Securitate within 24 hours. Romanians are forbidden from hosting foreign citizens if they are not close family.

1986 – In March, Mikhail Gorbachev presents his perestroika and glasnost theses in Moscow; minimum wage abolished, payment based on accomplishments.

1987 – Mihai Pacepa's book Red Horizon is published, revealing the side scenes of the Ceausescu regime; workers' revolt in Brasov.

1988 – Program for the organization of villages; annual per capita rations.

1989 – The New York Times (March 10) publishes the letters of the 6 old guard communists – Parvulescu, Gh. Apostol, C. Manescu, S. Brucan, G. Raceanu and A. Barladeanu – asking Ceausescu to change his domestic policy; the revolt in Timisoara (December 16).; on December 25, the Ceausescus are lined up against the wall of an outhouse and shot by an execution squad in Targoviste.

SIDEBAR 1

Psychological profile

He was an isolated individual (he had no friends, the only person he relied on being his wife), fierce and angry, critical with his employees.

By Psychologist Roxana Dobri.

His mother did not have enough strength to love and protect him. His alcoholic and irresponsible father's aggressiveness scarred him for life. Nicolae would always avoid this fatherly model, looking for a "good" father to protect him and offer him security. Since he could not find such a person, he turned into the Romanian people's "Father".

Because of his parents' relationship, Ceausescu was destined from early childhood to become an ambivalent individual. He was in his element in the conflict between the US and USSR. He defied

74

Russia's authority, in fact defying the paternal authority. He turned into the rebel adolescent who denied his parents – i.e. those who had built Communism in the world, including Romania – in order to "throw himself" into the arms of a family at odds with his own – i.e. the West.

The anger and helplessness that characterized his early years, his youth in capitalist Bucharest, were sublimated in the frenzy of grandeur that was going to be sustained progressively by the whole country.

He hid his frustrations and humiliation well, gaining power, gradually but surely, first at home and then on an international level. The system he promoted supported the myth of self-achievement, the rule according to which he overcame his own life history without ever escaping it – promoting peasants' and poor workers' children (like himself). His childhood limitations and poverty probably drove him to the creation of "the New Man," a humble and ascetic socialist.

Preparing his ascent to the top of the Party, many years before, Nicolae Ceausescu relied on unquestionable qualities. He manifested signs of excellent emotional intelligence abilities that helped him take his destiny into his own hands right from the moment he arrived in Bucharest.

Joining the Romanian Communist Party was the only way he could achieve acknowledgement and rapid social ascension. He was servile and submissive to Gheorghe Gheorghiu Dej, who would grant him access to the communist networks of the time. His abilities to negotiate convinced the old Party members that he was the most suitable successor to Dej. His capacity to seduce and convince through humility and submission, to dissimulate, helped him seize power in Romania.

In reality, he proved to be emotionally unstable, acting without thinking of the consequences of his own deeds. He was an isolated individual (he had no friends, the only person he relied on being his wife), fierce and angry, critical and evaluating with his employees.

His non-verbal behavior during his speeches from the podium or balcony shows a man who is rigid, limited, tormented by his own need to control his speech impediments and his emotions and to be accepted and flattered by the crowd. These were not the personal characteristics of a man who lived the delusive picture of total power and the need to be worshipped, a need satisfied year after year by the millions of people who chanted his name for minutes on end.

Some observers of the time thought that Ceausescu lived in a parallel universe, trying to explain the fact that the hard life of the Romanian people in the '90s was caused by the Party machine and not by the dictator's decisions. I believe that world was the universe that Ceausescu consciously wanted and created – in a socio-political environment that facilitated the delirium of his grandeur – according to the mental pathology with which he lived.

SIDEBAR 2

Grand Legacies

Ceausescu's 7 Obsessions – why he built them and what's happend to them

By Andreea Campeanu

I did something for this country! The People's House beats the Taj Mahal! - said Ceausescu to architect Anca Petrescu. Perseverant and tenacious in his centralizing megalomania, Ceausescu wanted to build as much as possible, on the largest scale possible, in order to show how much power the Romanian people had.

1. The People's House (The Palace of Parliament)

Goal: To show the world what the Romanians were capable of; he would gather the state leadership institutions in one place.

78

Construction: It was built in only 5 years by an army of 400 architects and 20,000 construction workers, sacrificing one fifth of the historic areas of Bucharest. Only Romanian materials were used. The bill: $2 billion; work continued for 7 years after Ceausescu's death.

Today: The second largest administrative building in the world, after the Pentagon in Washington; 332,000 sq m (3,573,600 sq ft); houses the Parliament, the Constitutional Court, the Official Gazette, the International Convention Center, the National Museum of Contemporary Art, conference halls, restaurants, and clubs.

2. The Transfagarasan (DN 7C)

Goal: Planned as a strategically important road for the passage of Romanian armored cars in case of an attack on the western front.

Construction: Built in 4 years (1970 – 1974); dynamited three times a day; has a maximum altitude of 2,042 m (6,700 ft), length of 91.5 km (56.8 mi), and a tunnel 887 m (2,910 ft) long. Built primarily by a military workforce.

Today: Tourist attraction during the summer; closed from October through June due to snow; currently in bad condition.

3. Hunger Circuses (Agro-alimentary Complexes)

Goal: Were to be large canteens for residents of Bucharest, eliminating their need to cook at home.

Construction: Began at the end of the 1980s; in 1989, only two "circuses" were finished.

Today: After 1989, they were abandoned; later turned into malls or modern commercial complexes.

4. The Danube – Black Sea Canal

Goal: Shortening the way to the Port of Constanta by approximately 400 km (248 mi).

Construction: Began in 1949, but was interrupted in 1955 and recommenced on June 13, 1973; inaugurated on May 26, 1984. 64 km (39.7 mi) long, 7 m (23 ft) deep, and 70 m (230 ft) wide. Cost: 2 billion euros; the recuperation of the investment was predicted to take 50 years.

Today: The third largest construction of its kind, after the Suez and Panama canals. The canal brings in an average of 3,160,000 euros annually: the investment can be repaid in 633 years.

5. The Bucharest Subway

Goal: Smoother traffic in the capital.

Construction: Intense pace; problems insulating the tunnels; the first sections were dug as ditches on the banks of the Dambovita river, later covered with concrete; construction began on February 3, 1975; the first section went into use in November of 1979.

Today: 75 km (46.6 mi) long; 50,000 passengers/hour is the maximum capacity, circa 50 trains (on average 300,000 passengers/day).

6. Casa Radio

Goal: Ceausescu wanted to bring all of Romania's museums under one roof as a museum of the Communist Party, a Trajan's column; planned to have seven floors.

Construction: Began in 1986; would have been finished in 1992; the second largest building in Bucharest after the House of the People; 110,000 sq m (1,184,000 sq ft); basement finished, ground floor almost finished; it took a long time because Ceausescu kept coming up with new ideas.

Today: Contracted for 49 years to Turkish investors; 70% of it will be demolished and remodeled; 450 million-euro investment; ready in 8 years; there will be stores, a hotel, offices, casinos: Dambovita Center.

7. The National Library

Goal: A central location for the National Library of Romania; a depository of books in a single place.

Construction: Began in 1986; 57,000 sq m (613,500 sq ft); in 1990, the funds for its finalization were redistributed.

Today: book depository; has undergone remodeling for 33 months, keeping its communist façade.

SIDEBAR 3

Whose House Is It Anyway?

By Justin Kavanagh

E veryone's mood changed once we entered the Palace of the Parliament. Ceausescu's House. Or the People's House, I never figured out which it really was. But the warm, hospitable Romanians that I'd been with for 24 hours suddenly seemed shrouded in shame and bitterness.

I remembered that sinister greeting from the Irishman's novel:

"Welcome to my house. Come freely. Go safely; and leave something of the happiness you bring."

Like the legend of Dracula, this egregious edifice was imposed on this country, and has since become an unwelcome part of the landscape. If Romania is known to the outside world as the

83

home of Dracula and Ceausescu, the people here are decidedly ambiguous about both unsolicited legacies.

Like the Count's infamous welcome, our tour of the Palace of the Parliament embodied the dark duality that seems to pervade many things Romanian; a smiling public facade failing to hide some badly masked menace from a knowing people.

We shuffled silently through the security scanner. Once inside, we were herded together by our tour guide. In the first of many grand, anonymous halls, my Romanians hosts told me that this wasn't officially called the People's House any more. That was the unofficial name. Originally the House of the Republic, it had become the House of Ceausescu, a name of shame adapted for a few years back in the early 1990s. Back then, when the ghost of the dictator might have been exorcised from its 1,100 rooms, the people might have reclaimed this citadel that was still being completed with their blood, sweat, and lei.

Now they were outsiders again. The Palace was more or less complete, but strangely vacant. Now the Romanians paid, along with foreigners like me, for a tour of the house that had now transmogrified into The Palace of the Parliament. Almost twenty years after the revolution, it's back to being "The Politicians' House," I thought.

The world sees Romanians in a heroic light, as the brave citizens who drove a stake into the heart of the Ceausescu regime in this very place. Yet one of my hosts was now telling me that for Romanians, the real national narrative is the story of Miorita; that their role is that of the passive Moldavian shepherd in the ballad of the Little Sheep. Passive acceptance is still the accepted lot of the people.

We followed the bright, young voice around the vast passages and the empty, echoing halls of the Palace of the Parliament. There was something extremely sinister about the tour. The pleasant young woman with perfect English gave us all the facts and all the superlatives of a building that reflects all the rampant egomania of its creator: we were standing in the most expensive administrative building in the world; the building contained one million cubic meters of marble from Transylvania; it housed 480 chandeliers; 200,000 square meters of woolen carpets; the velvet and brocade curtains, adorned with embroideries, were among the longest in the world; one of Europe's biggest chandeliers was in another part of the building, where we wouldn't be going today.

All very interesting and edifying, but one simple fact was missing from the tour, strangled in the screaming silence that followed these fantastic fact checks: this building was the bricks and mortar of a dictator's dream. We were standing in the fantasy palace of Europe's most brutal dictator since Hitler and Stalin.

I wanted to know who mined all this endless marble that lined the wall, and what that cost in human terms. Instead we got a guided tour, presented as a dictatorship Disneyland by numbers. A lot of fascinating figures about interior decorating, but barely a word about one of the greatest political dramas of late 20th Century Europe. The details were as sparse as the furnishings of the great empty rooms we hiked around diligently. Seeing nothing. Learning even less. There was nothing to see in these rooms except space. We were told about the size of the main offices upstairs, but no mention was made of the Ceausescus' desperate escape through these rooms to the helicopter on the rooftop.

In the anodyne tone of tour-guides everywhere, the young woman fed us these endless figures and meaningless measurements. What did it tell us about the people who had to build it? Nothing. There was no mention of the people displaced to build this place.

I heard later that Bucharest's wild dog problem started in earnest due to the upheaval caused to the neighborhoods razed for the Palace of the Parliament and for Union Boulevard. Marble halls for the powerful, gauntlets of rabid dogs for the poor. Such details remained the untold legacy of the dictator.

The tour did achieve its purpose though. It sent the visitor away impressed by the sheer scale of the construction. The empty monotony and lack of imagination of everything about the place made a dull impression too. "This is what you get when you give a peasant from Oltenia endless possibilities," whispered one of my hosts.

The real shock of that day for an outsider, however, was the visceral reaction of the Romanians themselves, the chilled shift from their spirited demeanor. Inside these walls, they seemed to trudge through their hidden history under a gloom. It was like witnessing a haunting.

Clearly, the past still lingered in these rooms. But what of the present and what of the future? I decided to ask the obvious question: "Why is this place so empty?" Where else in the world would one find these acres of empty floor space inside such a well-constructed building at the very heart of a capital city? Why not put all this valuable real estate to practical use?

I was given a quick historic recap of the many previous plans for the building: proposed home of an alternative World Bank; planned home for the Presedintia Republicii (Romanian Presidency), Marea Adunare Nationala (Great National Assembly), Consiliul de Ministri (Government Ministries) and Tribunalul Suprem (Supreme Court)—this was the original plan under Ceausescu; after the revolution, a site for a multinational casino; there was even a debate about razing it to the ground in order to banish the phantom of the dictator, a solution which would merely have compounded the public insult of this black hole in the Romanian economy.

So, to assuage the hurt, the House of the People became known for a spell after the revolution as the House of Ceausescu. Nowadays, it is home to the Senate and the Chamber of Deputies, as well as the site of the National Museum of Contemporary Art (MNAC), and the Museum and Park of Totalitarianism and Socialist Realism. Yet most of the rooms we saw in it were empty.

So why not use all this wasted space? How many NATO summits can there be on the calendar to fill up its vast corridors, its grand halls, and its echoing conference rooms? If the House of the People was not the de facto House of the Politicians, why not open more of it to the public to use as they see fit?

The answer to that question came from my friend Catalin (Gruia): "The public doesn't use it, Justin, because the public doesn't really belong here. We got rid of one Ceausescu and replaced him with a hundred little Ceausescus."

The spirit of oppressed passivity that Ceausescu inspired in Romanians seemed to prevail in that cold, brightly lit yet foreboding place. His legacy lived on there. "The Great Architect" was one of the many accolades his propaganda machine bestowed upon him. "Defender of the present and the future" was another.

Inside the citadel today, one still hears the wind rattling through doors and windows, which were never properly installed. It's a fitting reminder that no amount of power or wealth can fully insulate a leader from the outside world.

88

Now the world was coming in as tourists, walking through the small part of his world that we were allowed to see. We stopped to take in the Grand Hall, with its large empty space in the wall originally intended for a large painting of "The Polyvalent Genius" (who made up this stuff?). This endless monument to megalomania was now pushing the limits of my patience.

We trooped on into another ornate hall, with another plush pile carpet. Then something very interesting happened. Andreea, the youngest of our group, got bored and, in the casual way of her generation (the post-revolutionary Romanians) dropped herself and her rucksack and her camera in the middle of a main hallway and simply sprawled out on the floor. I waited for the inevitable guard, the outraged lackey in uniform chastising her lack of respect.

I wondered how long one could make oneself comfortable on the carpets of the Senate Building in Washington, say, or the palace at Versailles, before the wrath of officialdom would descend with all its fusty force. Tired too of this tour, I joined her on the carpet. If nothing else, being horizontal gave one a good look at the opulently decorated ceilings. They were a long way up. I wondered how many stories were contained in the buildings razed to make this one.

Soon we were all on the carpet. No guard ever came. Security here is just another façade, I thought. The guards know that all they are guarding is a vacant space at the heart of Bucharest.

They are making a show of guarding the void that represents modern Romania's soul.

I later learned that two neighborhoods including numerous Christian Orthodox and Protestant churches, synagogues and Jewish temples, and 30,000 homes, were sacrificed to make way for Ceausescu's house. A football stadium was interred in its foundations. Although all the construction is now more or less complete, Bucharesters are still living with the fallout of this Ceaushima; and all Romanians are still living through the half-lives of Nicolae Ceausescu.

He is Romania's modern-day Dracula, the Undead, still draining the life force of his people. Still alive in the collective memory, still poisoning their politics with his lingering legacy. It is the politicians, after all, who still have the only set of keys to the big house on the hill.

Lying there on the comfortable carpet in his "House of the People," I wondered what those people felt about the place now. It is a question I'd like to ask them: what would you do if you were given the keys to the House of the People? No doubt the dictator would have chased such an act of flagrant imagination out of his building. But it is no longer his building. Or is it?

The House of the People has 236.1/190.8 meters, covering an area of 44,000 square meters. It ranks second on the list of the biggest administrative buildings in the world, after The Pentagon. Demolishment works completed so as to clear the ground for building this structure covered 50 hectares. Constructors, workers and soldiers were swarming on the yard site. During peak periods, there were close to 20,000 people working here, in 3 shifts.

Photo by Andrei Pandele.

SIDEBAR 4

The Green Bananas and the Yellow Oranges of the Red Times

By George Hari Popescu, Journalism teacher,
Cyberculture.ro

"So how exactly are we going to split everything between the three of us now?" I once asked my parents, while we were all sitting at the table. Our baby brother had by then become big enough to eat oranges and bananas, too. It had been easier with only me and my sister: we shared by breaking everything in half, even the chocolates we got for some classmate's birthday, at school. But oranges and bananas were too precious, and I was really worried by the prospect of having my rightful part diminished.

Y ou could find plenty of bananas and oranges in every shop after the Revolution. I guess they had also been stored in warehouses

92

during the communist years, but the strict planning of food ratios had not allowed those in charge with their distribution to sell them on the market. You could only find these famous fruits for sale around Christmas, and only in very limited amounts. This is why oranges and bananas have always made me think of Christmas.

In order to get them, we had to go to a shop behind our block of flats. Once we bought them, the green bananas were wrapped in newspapers and placed somewhere high, up on some wardrobe. Rumors had it that if you wrapped them and kept them warm, they ripened faster. Sometimes we used to do the same with oranges that were a mere yellow when we were buying them.

There was a whole ritual designed for eating your bananas and oranges. You did not eat them all at once; you always had to keep another piece for the next day. If you were left with only one banana or one orange, you just ate half of it, in order to still save something for the following day. I was lucky enough to also like the taste of orange peel, so I had more days when I could actually bask in this delight.

When they were ripe, oranges had a bright color and a wonderful smell, so we used them as ornaments for our Christmas tree. We made some nicks on their peel and inserted some sewing thread in there, then popped them on the tree branches! They were our most precious Christmas decorations.

And do you know how we used to eat an orange back then? We were relishing every little bit of it! You had to master the art of making a small slice last as long as possible. And then for me, it was the same with a piece of the orange peel. To this day, I happily remember that stingy sensation on the tip of my tongue, when I was sinking my teeth in the orange wrinkly peel. Also, we used to let orange seeds dry up, to further keep them in fond remembrance for a while. Some parents were even dreaming of planting those seeds in the ground, in the countryside, hoping to grow orange trees one day! Naivety pushed up to the edge of ridicule...

Another opportunity to get bananas and oranges was the Christmas festivity held at our parents' working place. My parents were both working in the Post Office – the place where we got gifts of goodies in plastic bags showing the face of Santa Claus, if we were able to nicely recite a poem. With the Union's money, the Post Office was buying chocolate, waffles, specially wrapped chocolate bonbons for the Christmas tree, puffed corn snacks and last but not least, oranges! And if I'm not wrong, there used to be two oranges per plastic bag, and I was getting two bags because both my parents were working in the same place.

For a few months after the Revolution, the taste of bananas and oranges kept reminding me of Christmas. I talked to my girlfriend about that two days ago, and she said she still remembered Christmas whenever she was eating any of the two fruits. I stopped making this connection, although back then, a few months after the Revolution, I was still making it. However, my girl is younger than me. I wonder if she still remembers that because she is closer to that moment. Or is it perhaps because in the meantime I have also tasted other fruits of democracy?

I just feel like I've been deprived of an exclusivist thing. I can now eat as many bananas and oranges as I please. However, their taste does not remind me of that period of time anymore. Ultimately, I guess this is what 'leaving your childhood behind' actually means.

The End

A black dog licks at a puddle of blood in which two old people lie, executed on Christmas day in the Targoviste garrison. Following a kangaroo trial, a special tribunal sentenced them to death by shooting in December 1989 for "serious crimes against the people of Romania." He died instantly. The woman died a minute later, after the execution squad's paratroop captain furiously emptied another round in her. Thus Nicolae and Elena Ceausescu's five-decade journey together ended, after they started from the bottom, seized power, and grew old while ruling the country.

Adulated for all of his 24 years in power, during which he came to personify Romania, Ceausescu – dethroned and replaced by some of his former barons – was turned into a scapegoat for all the evils done to Romanians.

During his regime, Ceausescu's image had been painted in sparkling white. Once he was killed – everything turned to pitch black. I tried my best to paint a portrait in color, with all shades of grey included, combining the good and bad, the light and the dark extremes of the life of Nicolae Ceausescu.

Romania has changed a lot since his death. Although it's only been a quarter of a century, Ceausescu's age is an oddity to the young people in my generation and almost incomprehensible to the younger.

To us Romanians, embracing successive, opposite models in our civilization is nothing short of a historical tradition. Despite being halfway between the Atlantic and the Urals on the map, Romanian land has always lain at the outskirts of the great political and civilization structures.

According to historian Lucian Boia, "Romania's permanent frontier condition led to both isolation and permeability to influences from all directions. Relating to different, often conflicting foreign models – the Byzantine, then the Ottoman (in the Middle Ages), the Occidental (in the 19th century and the first half of the 20th), the Eastern (the second half of the 20th century) and again the Occidental at present – has given Romania an unstable, contradictory history."

Today, we live in a form-without-content kind of democracy – chaotic, unstructured. Those who are maladjusted to the new market economy don't know how to manage on their own and feel increasingly nostalgic thinking of the times when the Good Father made sure they have a roof over their head, food on their table, a job a.s.o. And there's more and more of them. The danger of a new dictator in Romania is real, what with our habit of hopping from one extreme to the other.

Of course, I couldn't stop that, not to mention it would be completely absurd to try to. But I can give you a crash course in all I know about Ceausescu.

About the Author

Catalin Gruia is a veteran journalist who has written and reported for the Romanian edition of National Geographic for over 10 years. He is currently Editor in Chief of National Geographic Traveler and Deputy Editor in Chief of National Geographic Romania.

International awards

☐ **First prize (Geographica section)** at the International Seminar of National Geographic International Editions, Washington, 2004

☐ **Johann Strauss Golden Medal**, Vienna, 2010.

☐ **Kinarri Trophy**, Friends of Thailand Awards, Bangkok, 2013.

Made in the USA
Coppell, TX
04 September 2022

82615672R00059